D1243116

MIGHTY MACHINES
Race Cars

by Derek Zobel

BLASTOFF! READERS

BELLWETHER MEDIA • MINNEAPOLIS, MN

Note to Librarians, Teachers, and Parents:

Blastoff! Readers are carefully developed by literacy experts and combine standards-based content with developmentally appropriate text.

Level 1 provides the most support through repetition of high-frequency words, light text, predictable sentence patterns, and strong visual support.

Level 2 offers early readers a bit more challenge through varied simple sentences, increased text load, and less repetition of high-frequency words.

Level 3 advances early-fluent readers toward fluency through increased text and concept load, less reliance on visuals, longer sentences, and more literary language.

Level 4 builds reading stamina by providing more text per page, increased use of punctuation, greater variation in sentence patterns, and increasingly challenging vocabulary.

Level 5 encourages children to move from "learning to read" to "reading to learn" by providing even more text, varied writing styles, and less familiar topics.

Whichever book is right for your reader, Blastoff! Readers are the perfect books to build confidence and encourage a love of reading that will last a lifetime!

This edition first published in 2010 by Bellwether Media, Inc.

No part of this publication may be reproduced in whole or in part without written permission of the publisher. For information regarding permission, write to Bellwether Media, Inc., Attention: Permissions Department. Post Office Box 19349, Minneapolis, MN 55419.

Library of Congress Cataloging-in-Publication Data
Zobel, Derek, 1983–
  Race cars / by Derek Zobel.
     p. cm. – (Blastoff! readers. Mighty machines)
  Includes bibliographical references and index.
  Summary: "Simple text and full color photographs introduce beginning readers to race cars. Developed by literary experts for students in kindergarten through grade 3"–Provided by publisher.
  ISBN 978-1-60014-193-5 (hardcover : alk. paper)
  1. Automobiles, Racing–Juvenile literature. I. Title.
  TL236.Z63 2010
  629.228–dc22
                        2009008276

Contents

A race car is
a fast machine.
It races
other cars.

A race car has
a powerful
engine.
It helps the
car reach
fast speeds.

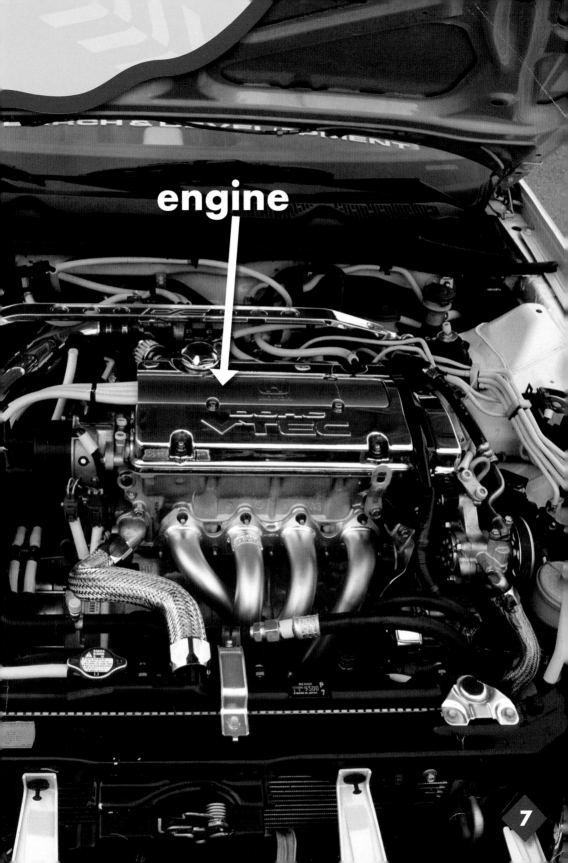

engine

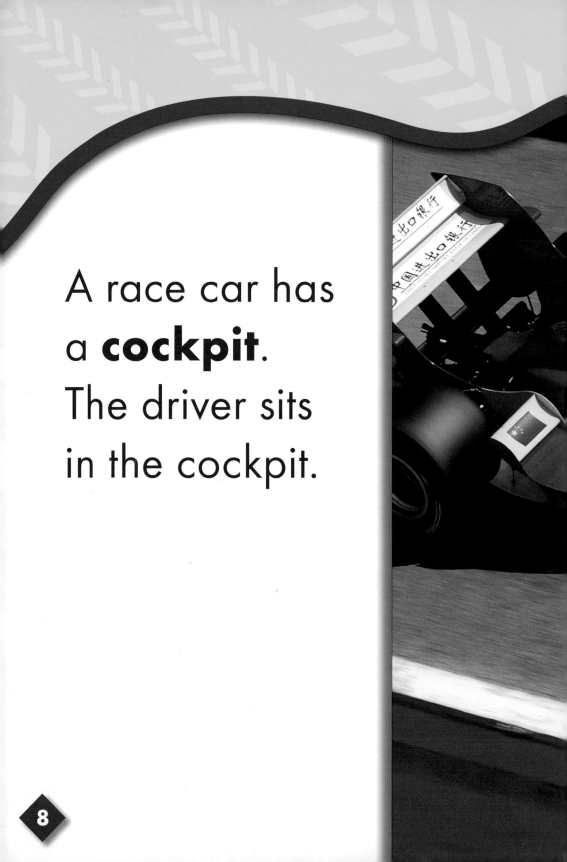

A race car has a **cockpit**. The driver sits in the cockpit.

cockpit

A race car
with a roof
has a **roll cage**.
This protects
the driver
in a crash.

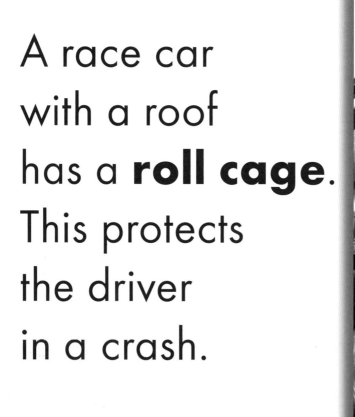

roll cage

Some race cars have **wings**. Wings help a driver stay in control.

wing

There are
many kinds
of race cars.
A **dragster**
is long and
skinny.

A **Formula One car** has smooth tires to grip the track.

A **rally car** has two racers inside. One drives and the other gives directions.

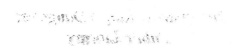

This **off-road** race car is built to race on dirt. Look at it go!

Glossary

cockpit—the place in a race car where the driver sits

dragster—a long, skinny race car with a powerful engine

engine—a machine that makes a vehicle move

Formula One car—a single-seat, open-cockpit race car

off-road—built to race on dirt and rock

rally cars—race cars made to race on public roads

roll cage—a set of metal bars that protects racers during a crash

wings—the parts of a race car that use wind to help a driver stay in control

To Learn More

AT THE LIBRARY

Jefferis, David. *Race Cars*. Chicago, Ill.: Raintree, 2003.

Rex, Michael. *My Race Car*. New York, N.Y.: Henry Holt & Co., 2000.

Zane, Alexander. *The Wheels on the Race Car*. New York, N.Y.: Scholastic, 2005.

ON THE WEB

Learning more about mighty machines is as easy as 1, 2, 3.

1. Go to www.factsurfer.com.

2. Enter "mighty machines" into the search box.

3. Click the "Surf" button and you will see a list of related Web sites.

With factsurfer.com, finding more information is just a click away.

Index

The images in this book are reproduced through the courtesy of: Creation Photography, front cover; Graham Bloomfield, p. 5; Ron Kimball/KimballStock, p. 7; STU, p. 9; Razvan CHIRNOAGA, p. 11; Rafa Irusta, p. 13; AP Images, p. 15; Eric Gevaert, p. 17; Tania Joubert, p. 19; Luis Louro, p. 21.